HODGE, DEBORAH.
BEAVERS /
C1998.
37565003376059 PETA

SONOMA COUNTY
LIBRARY
OFFICIAL
DISCARD

W9-BMN-903

Damage Noted
p. 12 torn, mended

Beavers

Written by Deborah Hodge

Illustrated by Pat Stephens

KIDS CAN PRESS

WILDLIFE SERIES

Kids Can Press

For Megan, Melanie and Rachel - DH
To Jasmine - PS

I would like to gratefully acknowledge the review of my manuscript by Barry Saunders, Registered Professional Biologist, wildlife consultant and former biologist with the British Columbia Ministry of Environment, Lands and Parks.

Thanks are also due to my trusty editor, Valerie Wyatt, my award-winning publishers, Ricky Englander and Valerie Hussey, and to Karen Michaluk for her unflagging enthusiasm and warmth.

Text copyright © 1998 by Deborah Hodge
Illustrations copyright © 1998 by Pat Stephens

All rights reserved. No part of this publication may be reproduced, stored in a retrieval system or transmitted, in any form or by any means, without the prior written permission of Kids Can Press Ltd. or, in case of photocopying or other reprographic copying, a license from CANCOPY (Canadian Copyright Licensing Agency), 6 Adelaide Street East, Suite 900, Toronto, ON, M5C 1H6.

We acknowledge the support of the Canada Council for the Arts and the Ontario Arts Council for our publishing program.

Published in Canada by
Kids Can Press Ltd.
29 Birch Avenue
Toronto, ON M4V 1E2

Published in the U.S. by
Kids Can Press Ltd.
85 River Rock Drive, Suite 202
Buffalo, NY 14207

Canadian Cataloguing in Publication Data

Hodge, Deborah
   Beavers

(Kids Can Press wildlife series)
Includes index
ISBN 1-55074-429-1

1. Beavers — Juvenile literature. I. Stephens, Pat. II. Title. III. Series.

QL737.R632H63 1998   j599.37
C98-930344-6

Edited by Valerie Wyatt
Designed by Marie Bartholomew
Printed in Hong Kong by Book Art Inc, Toronto

CM 98 0 9 8 7 6 5 4 3 2 1

Contents

Beavers are wild

Beavers are wild animals that live in ponds, lakes and streams. They are strong swimmers and graceful divers.

Beavers are mammals. Mammals have lungs and furry bodies. The babies drink their mother's milk.

Like all mammals, the beaver is warm-blooded. Its body temperature stays warm, even in icy water.

BEAVER
FACT

Beavers can
live for up to
12 years in
the wild.

Beavers are skillful builders. They cut down trees with
their long, sharp teeth. They float the trees through
water. They stack them to build large homes and dams.

Beavers are rodents

A beaver is a rodent – a mammal whose front teeth never stop growing. There are about 3000 kinds of rodents in the world. They include squirrels, chipmunks, rats, mice and porcupines.

Like the beaver, a few other rodents live in and around water. They are the capybara, nutria and muskrat. Although these rodents are like beavers in some ways, they are not closely related.

The muskrat lives in North America. It has a strong musky scent.

The beaver is the largest rodent in North America. An adult weighs from 16 to 32 kg (35 to 70 pounds) – as much as a large dog.

The nutria (also called the coypu) has a long, round tail. Nutrias are found in South America and the southern United States.

Like this beaver, all rodents chew on tough things to keep their teeth the right length. Beavers chew wood.

The capybara is the biggest rodent in the world – about the size of a small pig. It lives near rivers and ponds in South America.

Where beavers live

To survive, beavers need trees and water. Trees provide beavers with food and wood for building. Living in water helps them stay safe. If danger threatens, beavers can swim away.

Beavers are found in most wild areas of North America. Small numbers also live in Europe, Asia and at the tip of South America.

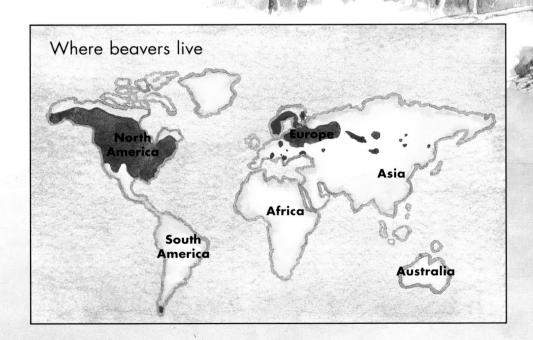

Where beavers live

North America

Europe

Asia

Africa

South America

Australia

BEAVER FACT

Millions of years ago, beavers lived in many northern parts of the world. Some were as big as bears.

Beavers live near woods, in streams, ponds or lakes. Each beaver family has its own home area. A family is often made up of parents, babies and older sisters and brothers.

Beaver food

Beavers are plant eaters. They feed on tree bark all year round. In spring and summer, they also eat new green plants.

Beavers have razor-sharp teeth for cutting trees. Special chemicals in their stomachs help them digest the bark. Their favorite trees are aspens or poplars. They also eat the bark from willow, birch and maple trees.

lodge

food pile

The beaver rolls a twig between its paws to eat the tasty bark.

BEAVER FACT

A beaver family cuts down hundreds of trees a year.

Every fall, beavers in northern areas store food for winter. They cut trees into small pieces, then stack the wood near their lodge. All winter long, they will eat from this food pile.

11

Beaver bodies

A beaver's body is strong. It is built for cutting and towing trees. In water, the beaver is sleek and graceful.

Tail

A beaver's tail is flat, scaly and about 30 cm (12 inches) long. Fat stored in the tail serves as food during winter.

Tail scales up close

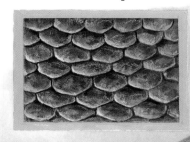

Oil glands

Two oils are stored in glands under the tail. The beaver uses one oil, called castoreum, to mark off its home area. It combs another oil into its fur to keep it waterproof.

Fe...

Web... ...ck feet help the beave... ...n. A double toenail is used to ...ombing the fur.

Eyes

Clear eyelids protect a beaver's eyes underwater. They let the beaver swim with its eyes open.

Ears and nose

Underwater, a beaver's ears and nose close over to keep water out.

Body fat

A thick layer of body fat keeps the beaver warm in cold water.

Fur

A beaver's long, soft fur protects it from insects, dirt and water. The color helps the beaver blend in with its surroundings.

Jaws and teeth

Powerful jaws and sharp front teeth bite into trees. Back teeth grind up the wood. A space between the front and back teeth is perfect for carrying sticks. Underwater, a flap of skin closes behind the front teeth. The flap keeps water out of the beaver's mouth.

How beavers move

The beaver's big back feet and powerful tail push it through the water. To speed up, the beaver pumps its tail hard. A fast-moving beaver can swim up to 10 km/h (6 miles per hour).

Webbed feet make it hard to walk on land.
The beaver's tail helps it balance.

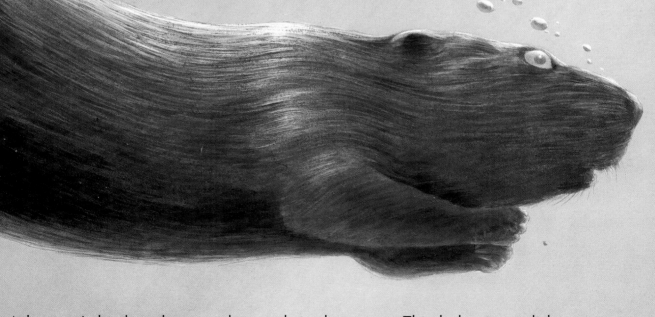

BEAVER FACT

A beaver can stay underwater for up to 15 minutes. Its heart slows down, so it needs less air.

A beaver's body is long and smooth in the water. This helps it to glide. Beavers often stay underwater for two or three minutes at a time.

A beaver dam

When beavers move into an area, they usually build a dam. The dam is like a wall across a stream. Water trapped behind it forms a deep pond. The beavers are safer in the deep water. Here they can build a home, store food and escape enemies.

1. The beavers wedge a row of sticks into the stream bed.

2. They weigh the sticks down with rocks and mud.

BEAVER FACT

Most dams are from 5 to 30 m (15 to 95 feet) long. Some are longer than a soccer field.

3. They pack branches and grasses between the sticks. They spread on mud to stop water coming through.

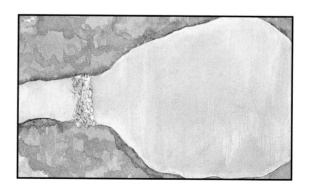

4. In two or three days, the dam is finished. The water behind the dam forms a deep pond.

A beaver lodge

A beaver home is called a lodge. Beavers build their lodge in the deep pond behind their dam. Like the dam, the lodge is made by piling up sticks, rocks and mud. It takes a pair of beavers about a week to build a lodge. They add to it and repair it often.

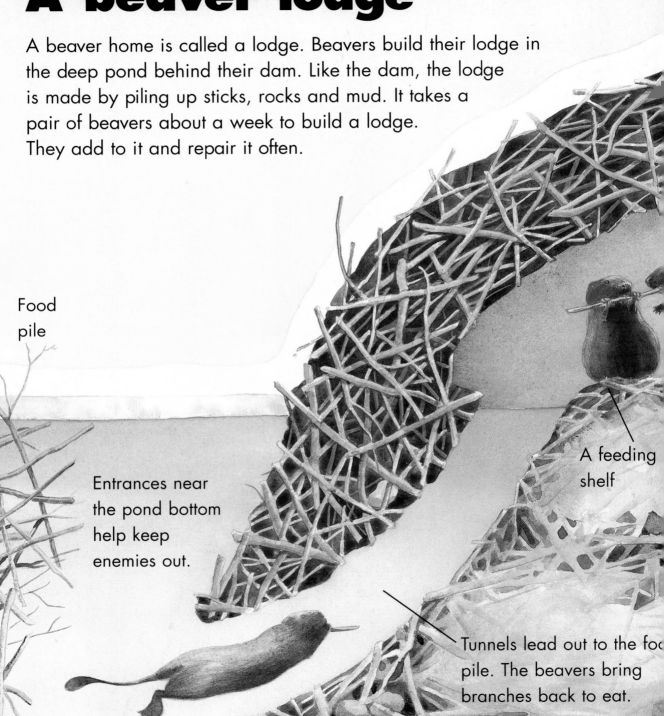

Food pile

Entrances near the pond bottom help keep enemies out.

A feeding shelf

Tunnels lead out to the food pile. The beavers bring branches back to eat.

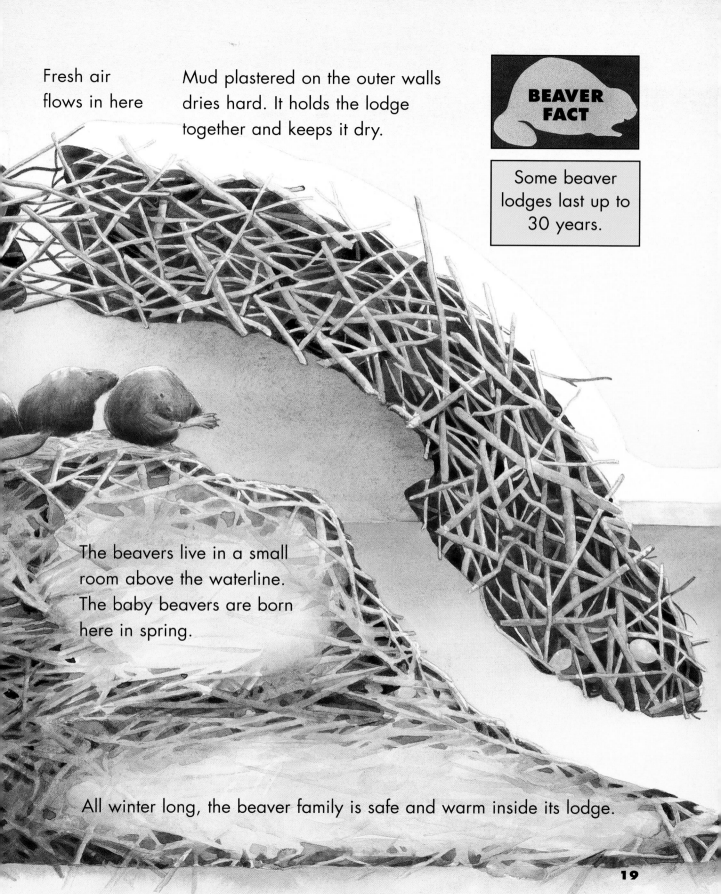

Fresh air flows in here

Mud plastered on the outer walls dries hard. It holds the lodge together and keeps it dry.

BEAVER FACT

Some beaver lodges last up to 30 years.

The beavers live in a small room above the waterline. The baby beavers are born here in spring.

All winter long, the beaver family is safe and warm inside its lodge.

How beavers are born

When a mother beaver is ready to give birth, the whole family helps clean the lodge. They spread leaves and grasses on the floor. On this fresh bed, the mother gives birth to three or four babies. The babies are called kits.

The newborn kits are covered with thick fur. Their eyes are open and their teeth are sharp. They look like tiny copies of their parents. As soon as they are born, the kits can see, hear, walk and swim.

A kit takes its first swim in the lodge tunnels. It can't waterproof its own fur yet, so the mother helps.

BEAVER
FACT

Beaver parents have a new litter of kits every spring. The whole family helps care for them.

Baby beavers drink their mother's rich milk. Like human babies, kits cry when they're hungry and coo when full.

How beavers grow and learn

At one month, the kits are ready to leave the lodge. They copy their mother and learn how to find food and stay safe.

By one year, the young beavers are strong enough to work. They cut trees and repair the dam or lodge. They help their parents care for a new litter of kits.

At age two, the young beavers leave their parents. They find mates and build their own lodges.

On land, a beaver may carry a kit in its paws.

BEAVER FACT

Unlike a human, a beaver keeps growing for as long as it lives.

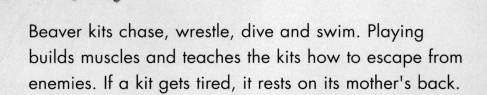

Beaver kits chase, wrestle, dive and swim. Playing builds muscles and teaches the kits how to escape from enemies. If a kit gets tired, it rests on its mother's back.

How beavers protect themselves

The beaver's main enemy is the otter. Otters can swim into the lodge through the underwater tunnels. They don't often attack adult beavers, but the kits are in great danger. Kits also fear eagles, hawks, owls and large fish.

A beaver has many enemies on land. Wolves, coyotes, foxes, bears, cougars, bobcats and lynx all hunt beaver. To protect itself, the beaver sniffs the air. It listens for danger. If enemies are near, the beaver will try to escape to water.

A loud tail slap warns that danger is near. Other beavers dive deep or quickly swim away when they hear the sound.

A cornered beaver will fight. Its strong jaws and sharp teeth become powerful weapons.

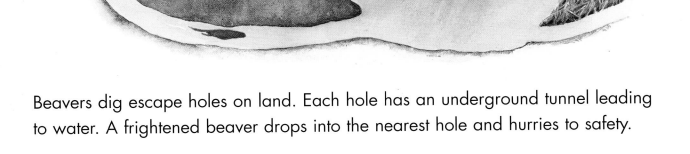

Beavers dig escape holes on land. Each hole has an underground tunnel leading to water. A frightened beaver drops into the nearest hole and hurries to safety.

Beavers in nature

Wherever beavers live, they change the land and water around them.

When beavers build a dam, a pond forms. The pond is home to birds, frogs, salamanders, insects and fish. Tree-cutting lets new plants grow in the forest. The plants feed rabbits, deer and other forest animals.

Once the food in an area is gone, the beavers move away. Their dam breaks down and water drains out of the pond. Rich soil is left behind. Soon a lush new meadow grows where the pond used to be.

Beavers and people

Long ago, beavers were hunted until few were left. People made coats and hats from the beaver's fur. Their castoreum was used for perfume and medicine.

Today, there are laws to protect the beaver. Now beavers live in most wild areas of North America. They are also coming back in Europe and Asia.

When beavers live near people, problems sometimes arise. Roads or fields may get flooded when beavers build a dam.

Beavers need space to roam and raise their young. They depend on clean water and healthy trees.

Beaver signs

Tracks

The large beaver tracks across these pages are life-sized. How does your hand size compare?

Front paw

Back paw

Dam

Dams and lodges

Beavers make large stick piles in ponds and streams. A lodge has a rounded shape. A dam stretches across the water.

Lodge

Tree stumps

Beavers leave big tooth marks on the trees they cut down.

Scent mounds

Beavers dig up piles of mud and leaves near the water's edge. They drop castoreum on top. The scent tells other beavers to stay away.

Words to know

castoreum: a scented oil stored in glands under a beaver's tail

dam: a stick and mud wall built by beavers across a stream or river

lodge: a beaver home built of sticks and mud

kit: a baby beaver

mammal: a warm-blooded animal with fur covering, whose babies are born live and fed their mother's milk

mate: a male or female partner in a pair of beavers. A beaver and its mate live together and produce baby beavers.

rodent: an animal whose front teeth never stop growing

warm-blooded: having a warm body temperature, even when the air or water is cold

Index